A Note to Parents and Teachers

DK READERS is a compelling new reading programme for children, designed in conjunction with leading literacy experts, including Cliff Moon M.Ed., Honorary Fellow of the University of Reading. Cliff Moon has spent many years as a teacher and teacher educator specializing in reading and has written more than 140 books for children and teachers. He reviews regularly for teachers' journals.

Beautiful illustrations and superb full-colour photographs combine with engaging, easy-to-read stories to offer a fresh approach to each subject in the series. Each DK READER is guaranteed to capture a child's interest while developing his or her reading skills, general knowledge, and love of reading.

The four levels of DK READERS are aimed at different reading abilities, enabling you to choose the books that are exactly right for your child:

Level 1 – Beginning to read
Level 2 – Beginning to read alone
Level 3 – Reading alone
Level 4 – Proficient readers

The "normal" age at which a child begins to read can be anywhere from three to eight years old, so these levels are intended only as a general guideline.

No matter which level you select, you can be sure that you are helping children learn to read, then read to learn!

LONDON, NEW YORK, MUNICH,
MELBOURNE AND DELHI

Project Editors Mary Atkinson
and Penny Smith
Art Editor Karen Lieberman
Senior Editor Linda Esposito
Production Kate Oliver
Picture Researchers Andy Sampson
and Kathy Lockley
Illustrator Peter Dennis

Reading Consultant
Cliff Moon M.Ed.

Published in Great Britain by
Dorling Kindersley Limited
80 The Strand, London WC2R 0RL
A Penguin Company

8 10 9

Copyright © 1998 Dorling Kindersley Limited, London

A CIP catalogue record for this book is
available from the British Library.

ISBN 978-0-7513-5715-8

Colour reproduction by Colourscan, Singapore
Printed and bound in China by L Rex Printing Co., Ltd.

The publisher would like to thank the following
for their kind permission to reproduce their photographs:
c=centre; t=top; b=below; l=left; r=right

AKG London Ltd: Erich Lessing 12tl; The Ancient Art and
Architecture Collection: Ronald Sheridan 3b, 17bl, 20t;
Bridgeman Art Library, London: Egyptian National Museum 17cla;
Louvre/Giraudon 7bcr; by kind permission of the Trustees of the
British Museum: 4tl, cl, 5tr, br, 6cl, 7tr, 8–9bc, 8tl, bl, 9tr, cr, 10l,
12bl, 13cr; Bruce Coleman Collection: Joe McDonald 18tl;
Colorific!: Kirsten P. Head 14cl; Mary Evans Picture Library: 20tl;
Forhistorisk Museum, Moesgard, Denmark: 4–5b; Robert Harding
Picture Library: 15tr, 16cl, 17b, tr; Walter Rawlings 17cl;
Michael Holford: 12b; Hulton Getty Collection: 14tl, 16tl;
Pelizaeus-Museum, Hildesheim, Germany: 7c, cb; Reunion des
Musées Nationaux: Louvre 11tr; Sygma: L'Illustration 19bl
All other images © Dorling Kindersley.
For further information see: www.dkimages.com

see our complete catalogue at
www.dk.com

Contents

DK READERS

PROFICIENT
4
READERS

SECRETS
OF THE MUMMIES

Written by Harriet Griffey

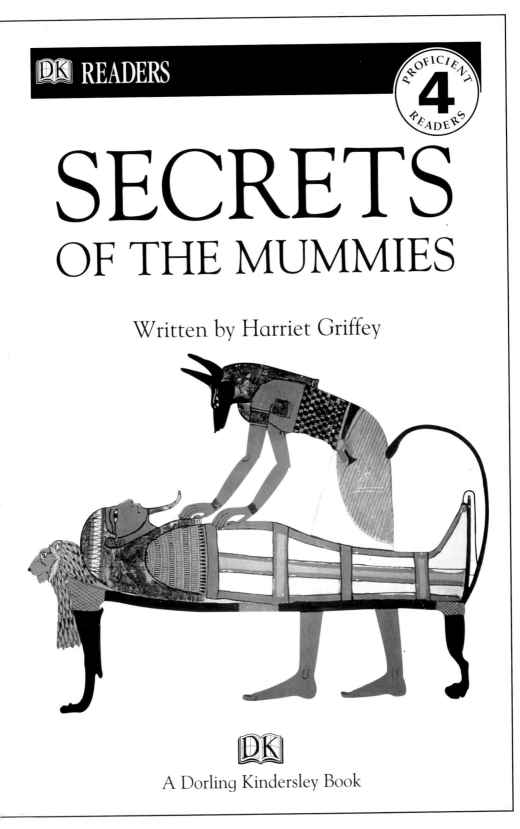

DK
A Dorling Kindersley Book

Teenage boy
Some Roman mummies were decorated with a realistic painting of the person who had died.

Animals
The ancient Egyptians believed cats were sacred. They often mummified cats' bodies when they died.

People from the past

There is something intriguing about a mummy. It is hard to believe that hundreds or even thousands of years ago it was a living person.

A mummy is the preserved body of someone who has died. The body may have been preserved naturally or deliberately as part of a religious ritual.

Naturally preserved bodies have been discovered in airless bogs. Here, the animals and bacteria that usually break down bodies cannot survive, so the body does not decay. This can also happen in hot, dry deserts and on icy mountains.

Other bodies were carefully preserved by people. The most famous mummies belong to the ancient Egyptians. But other cultures, such as the Incas of South America and the Pazyryks of Siberia, also used to preserve their dead. Some people buried their mummies with artefacts, such as bowls, statues and beautiful jewels.

This book investigates different mummies discovered around the world. But first, let us look at how the ancient Egyptians made a mummy.

This mummy was found in a Danish bog. It is the body of a man who died more than 1,500 years ago.

Artefacts
Everyday objects were often buried with mummies.

Important doll
Figures, such as this Peruvian doll, were buried with a mummy to bring the dead person luck in the afterlife.

5

A chief priest represented the king and the gods. He looked after a temple and performed certain rituals.

An Egyptian priest

Embalming
Chemicals, perfumes and balms are used in this process to stop a body from decaying.

Making a mummy

For 3,000 years, the ancient Egyptian civilization flourished. The people living then had strong beliefs about gods and life after death. They thought that if a dead person's spirit could recognize its preserved body, it would live forever in the afterlife.

Rich Egyptians paid the chief priests to mummify the bodies of their loved ones. They believed that the priests could help decide a person's fate after death.

"Come quickly," a servant would plead. "My master is dead."

Right away a chief priest would send a servant to summon other priests. They would be needed to help him embalm the body – a process that stops the body from decaying.

Then the chief priest would gather his tools and set off for his workshop on the west bank of the River Nile.

Meanwhile, other servants collected the body and carried it to the workshop. There they laid it on a special table, ready for the ceremony to begin.

The chief priest put on a jackal-headed mask to represent Anubis, the Egyptian god of mummification. Then he slowly washed the body while another priest read magic spells out loud. When the body was clean enough, the embalming process began.

Tools
These tools were used in a ritual intended to enable the mummy to eat and drink in the afterlife.

This ancient Egyptian painting shows a body being washed.

After being washed, the body was left to dry.

Jackal mask
At embalming ceremonies, jackal-headed masks, such as this pottery one, represented Anubis, god of mummification.

7

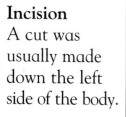

The chief priest picked up his embalming knife and carefully made a long cut down the left side of the body. Then he put his hand into the cut and pulled out the liver, lungs, stomach and guts. Each of these was stored in a canopic jar – a special container in the shape of a god.

The next part was difficult. He had to push a thin bronze hook up the dead person's nose and, bit by bit, scoop out the brain.

Incision
A cut was usually made down the left side of the body.

Embalming knife
This ceremonial knife has a sharp blade made of flint.

Hapy (HAR-pee) was a baboon god, who guarded the lungs.

The falcon god Qebehsenuef (KEB-EKH-SEN-OO-EF) guarded the intestines, or guts.

The brain was thrown away because the ancient Egyptians did not understand what it was for, so they did not think it was important.

After this the body was ready to be dried. The priests heaped natron, a natural salt, over the body to draw out all the fluids. It would take 40 days for the body to dry completely.

Only then would the body be ready for the next step.

Natron
This natural salt is found by the edges of desert lakes.

Stuffing
This X-ray of a mummy shows linen stuffing replacing some of the organs.

Sons of Horus
The four gods who guarded canopic jars were the sons of Horus, god of the sky.

Imsety (IM-SET-EE) was a human-like god who guarded the liver.

The jackal-headed god Duamutef (do-ar-MOOT-ef) guarded the stomach.

Magical figures
These figures lay on the body to guard the places where the organs had been removed.

Scarab beetle

Wadjet eye

Amulets
These were good luck charms. The wadjet eye was believed to keep away evil.

After 40 days, the dried body was filled with linen, sand or sawdust to help it keep its shape. Beeswax was pushed into the nostrils and linen was stuffed into the eye sockets. Next, oils and spices were rubbed into the skin to keep it from cracking.

Now the chief priest was ready to begin wrapping the body. He wound thin linen strips around each finger. Then he bandaged the arms and legs and the rest of the body.

Magical figures called amulets were wrapped in between the layers of cloth. At the same time, the priest brushed the bandages with resin to stick them together. Bandaging the body could take 15 days.

Finally the mummified body was placed in a coffin. If everything had gone well, the chief priest was pleased. All the dead person needed now was some magic spells.

Nest of coffins
Sometimes the coffin was put into a bigger coffin, which might then be put into an even bigger coffin, and so on.

Scribes
In ancient Egypt only scribes could write. They were highly respected people.

Scary figures
Figures like this hippo were put in the tomb to scare off intruders.

A scribe, or writer, handed the priests a scroll. The scroll was the "Book of the Dead" – a special book containing more than 200 spells. It was placed inside the coffin.

The ancient Egyptians believed that the dead person would need to recite the spells in the book to gain protection on his or her journey to the Hall of the Two Truths.

Hapy, the baboon god

The "Devourer of the Dead" waiting to eat the hearts of evil people.

Anubis, god of mummification

Feather of truth

Heart of the dead person

In this judgment hall, the great god Osiris was believed to watch over a ceremony when the dead person had to deny all his or her bad deeds.

Anubis, the jackal-headed god, used scales to balance the person's heart against the "feather of truth". If the heart was not too heavy with bad deeds, the dead person was allowed to live in the afterlife.

Back in this world, the dead person's family filled a tomb with food and treasures for the mummy to use in the afterlife. Curses were often written over the coffin and the walls of the tomb, warning intruders of terrible punishments for stealing.

But over the centuries grave robbers broke into the tombs looking for buried treasure. A legend grew that somewhere in the Egyptian Valley of the Kings lay a rich, untouched tomb – the tomb of the young king Tutankhamun. ❖

Underworld
It was thought that everyone passed through this land on their way to the afterlife. They began their journey by crossing the River Nile.

God of death
Osiris was king of the after-world, which was thought to be like Egypt but better.

Howard Carter
After travelling to Egypt as a young artist, Carter's interest turned to investigating ancient Egypt.

Pharaoh
The pharaohs were the kings of ancient Egypt. The people believed them to be living gods.

The mummy's curse

"I must find the lost tomb."

Howard Carter had been saying the same thing for years. Now it was 1922, the fifth year he had spent digging through sand and rocks in Egypt's Valley of the Kings. He was searching for a tomb that no grave robbers had ever found – the tomb of Tutankhamun, the boy pharaoh.

Carter scoffed when he was warned of the curse: "Death comes on wings to he who enters the tomb of a pharaoh."

Each day, his men worked in the sweltering heat and dust. They seemed to be getting nowhere. Then one morning, as they dug in soft rubble, a spade clanged.

When Carter arrived, he was met by an excited hush. The men had found a stone step. Another 15 steps were quickly uncovered. Could this be Tutankhamun's tomb?

Tutankhamun
This pharaoh ruled from around 1336 BC to 1327 BC. He was probably still a teenager when he died.

Valley of the Kings
To avoid grave robbers, many pharaohs chose this remote place for their tombs.

Carnarvon
This wealthy English lord visited Egypt for his health. His interest in tombs began as a way to pass the time.

Hieroglyphs
Each symbol in this ancient Egyptian writing stands for a word or a sound.

The staircase led to a sealed door. Carter wanted to open it but he had to wait. Lord Carnarvon, his patron, had paid for the years of work and wanted to be present at the opening.

Today it would take only six hours to reach Egypt from Carnarvon's home in England but at that time it took more than two weeks. When Carnarvon finally arrived, he hurried to the tomb. Nervously, he fingered the strange symbols, called hieroglyphs, by the door. Then he and Carter opened the door and crept inside.

The two men pushed their way through a rock-filled corridor, which led to another sealed door. Cautiously, they made a hole in the door.

Carter was the first to look. What he saw left him speechless. Later he told people that he had seen "strange animals, statues and gold – everywhere the glint of gold."

The room was untidily packed with priceless treasures. There were sparkling gems, animal-shaped beds, beautiful painted boxes and a magnificent golden throne.

Nothing had been touched for 3,000 years!

Wide-eyed, the pair picked their way through the riches. Then they came to a third sealed doorway. They were desperate to know where it led but again they had to wait. First, all these things had to be carefully sorted.

The paintings on this treasure chest show Tutankhamun conquering his enemies.

Tomb jewels
This vulture represented the goddess Nekhabet, and this scarab beetle ornament represented the sun god Khepri.

Afterlife of luxury
The ancient Egyptians filled the king's tomb with treasure, such as golden sandals and precious jewels, for him to use in the afterlife.

Kingly killer
While the cobra can kill people if disturbed, it also helps rid towns of rats and mice.

Royal dummy
Statues of Tutankhamun often show a cobra on his headdress. This wooden statue is a clothes dummy found in the tomb.

When Carter arrived home that night, his servants were wailing and shouting.

"What's wrong?" Carter demanded above the din.

"You have opened the tomb," wept a servant. "We are cursed!" He told Carter that a cobra had swallowed Carter's pet canary at the exact moment the tomb was opened. Cobras were a symbol of royalty in ancient Egypt. They were said to spit fire at a pharaoh's enemies.

Carter was not worried. The next day he began to clear the first room of the tomb.

More than a kilometre of cotton wadding was used to wrap up the items. Carter's team packed games, clothing, pottery, musical instruments and statues. Most of these were sent to Cairo, Egypt's capital, by boat. The more valuable artefacts went on a train accompanied by armed guards.

Finally the men were ready to unseal the third door. Slowly and carefully, Carter started chipping away the rocks and plaster. Then he stopped. Before him was a wall of solid gold! It was the front of a huge, golden shrine. Carter was astonished. He knew that this was the greatest ancient Egyptian find ever.

Cairo
Egypt's capital city grew up 1,000 years after the death of the last pharaoh.

Howard Carter (left) and his assistants carefully wrap a life-size statue.

Gold cabinet
This royal shrine filled nearly all of the third room.

Kingly coffin
The middle coffin was made of wood covered in gold with inlaid glass.

Inside the golden shrine were three more shrines. And inside the last one was a sarcophagus – a stone coffin. But that was not all. Within the sarcophagus were three more coffins, each fitting snugly inside the other. The final coffin was made of solid gold. Inside it was the mummified body of Tutankhamun.

But before anyone could investigate further, disaster struck. It began when Carter's patron, Lord Carnarvon, was bitten on the cheek by a mosquito.

He accidentally cut open the bite while shaving. The bite soon became infected and fever set in.

A few days later Carnarvon's family raced to his bedside. He was very ill. Then, early one morning, it was all over. Lord Carnarvon died.

At the very moment of his death, all the lights in Cairo went out. They stayed out for several hours and no-one could explain why. Back at Lord Carnarvon's home in England, Susie, his dog, pricked up her ears, howled once, then dropped dead.

Other deaths followed. A French scientist who visited the tomb died after a fall. An X-ray specialist on his way to examine Tutankhamun's mummy died unexpectedly. Then a wealthy American died from a virus after visiting the tomb. Were these deaths all coincidences or was the curse of the mummy to blame? No-one knows for sure. ❖

Deadly fever
Carnarvon's razor and death certificate are reminders of how deadly a simple cut could be in the days before antibiotics were invented.

Royal mummy
Although the riches in the tomb were in good condition, Tutankhamun's mummy was badly decayed.

Inca empire
This empire covered parts of what are now Colombia, Ecuador, Peru, Bolivia, Chile and Argentina.

Sun temples
Temples to the Sun god were built all over the empire.

Inca emperors

As dawn broke, drumbeats sounded through the city of Cuzco. The people began to wake and an excited buzz filled the air. It was the most important day of the year in the Inca empire – a civilization that covered much of South America 500 years ago.

Today was Inti Raimi, a religious festival held in honour of Inti, the Sun god. Every year, this festival was celebrated on 21 June – midwinter's day. By showing thanks and honouring Inti, the Inca people believed that summer would come once more and their crops would grow.

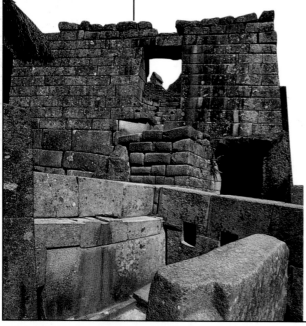

Temples were built from carefully shaped blocks of stone. Sun temples were often filled with solid gold models of cornstalks, lumps of earth and other things related to farming.

Everyone in the Inca empire gave one-third of all they produced to the priests of the Sun god. Many of these plants and animals were sacrificed in special ceremonies held throughout the year. Today's ceremonies were the most important of all.

Inca year
The Incas had a religious festival for each month. Inti Raimi was held in June, as this is the coldest month of the year in South America.

Sun disc
The Sun god was represented in many Inca temples by gold discs with human faces.

Priests began to chant in time with the drumbeats. In the Holy Square, a large crowd gathered. The people were excited but quiet and respectful. They were waiting for the Procession of the Living Dead.

Llamas
The llama is related to the camel. Llamas are still used in South America for wool, meat and transportation.

At last, the crowds spotted the white llamas that always led the procession. There were hundreds of llamas walking in lines, one after another.

Behind the llamas came a litter carrying the emperor, the Sapa Inca. Everyone in the crowd knelt down, hid their faces in their hands and prayed. Ordinary people were not allowed to look at the Sapa Inca.

Next came litters, or stretchers, bearing the mummified bodies of the long-dead former Sapa Incas.

Each mummy was worshipped as a son of the Sun god. It was thought that the living Sapa Inca received advice and help from these mummies.

Sometimes a child would sneak a look. He or she would glimpse the mummies, each draped in beautiful cloth woven from the soft wool of the vicuna, a relative of the llama.

But even a peeping child would not see the emperors' faces. They were covered with golden masks, which the priests believed would protect the emperors in the afterlife.

Litters
These beds or stretchers were used to carry the mummies in processions.

Huari mummy
The Huari people lived near Cuzco before the Incas. They too mummified their leaders.

Gods
Incas had great respect for their gods. They gave them offerings, such as statues, gold, animals and sometimes even people.

Chica
This alcoholic drink was made from corn.
It was stored in decorated clay jars.

The procession stopped at the Temple of the Sun, where more ceremonies began. It was a long day, full of prayer. The people thought that if they pleased the mummified Sapa Incas, they would please the Sun god.

In the evening, things became a little more festive. The city's inhabitants feasted on roasted llamas served with corn cakes and potatoes. The adults drank freshly brewed chica, an alcoholic drink. There was singing and dancing until late at night. But even during the feast, the Sun god was not forgotten. The very best food was put in front of the god's sons, the mummified emperors.

At the end of the day, the mummies were returned to the palaces where they had lived when they were alive. These palaces were still kept in order by specially chosen workers.

The workers fanned the air to keep flies off the mummies. They offered the mummies food and water when they felt it was needed. Most importantly, they delivered messages to the mummies and interpreted their replies.

The people believed that long-gone ancestors could give advice. It did not matter that these emperors were dead – they were still considered very powerful. ❖

After the Spaniards conquered the Incas in 1532, they built a church on the site of the old Temple of the Sun in Cuzco.

Mummified bodies
For more than 4,000 years, people across South America mummified their dead.

27

Look-alike
The goddess statue was made of gold and dressed in similar clothes to the girl.

Inca ice maiden

The climbers were weary. It had taken three days to reach the top of Nevado Ampato, a high mountain in the Peruvian Andes. The paths were steep and the air was thin, making it difficult to breathe. But finally the four priests reached their destination – the top of the icy ridge.

From packs tied to the llamas, they unloaded pots, food, figurines and a small statue of a goddess. Then they set up a small stone altar.

With the group of priests was a thirteen-year-old girl, the daughter of an important Inca family. Under a warm blanket, she wore a beautiful belted dress of rich yellow, purple and red wool.

One of the priests led the girl to the altar. She took off the blankets, and the priest draped a finely woven cloth over her shoulders. He fastened the cloth with a silver pin.

Finally, while chanting special prayers, the chief priest placed a large feathered headdress on the girl's head.

Headdress
The girl's headdress was made of macaw feathers. These feathers were often used in religious ceremonies.

Last resort
The Incas stored food in case of a famine. But if there was a long famine, the people appealed to the gods.

Llama herd
Statues were often used in ceremonies. This llama statue may have reminded the gods to provide grass for their herds to eat.

The unusual group had travelled to the mountain because of a severe three-year drought. Crops had failed and the people were starving. The priests believed that the drought was caused because the gods were angry.

After much prayer and talk, they had decided that a special sacrifice should be made to the mountain god – they must sacrifice someone who was almost perfect. Whoever was chosen would live forever with the gods in the afterlife. Such a sacrifice would surely please the gods and bring rain.

The girl and her family were a little frightened when she was chosen, but they also felt very honoured.

Now the girl sat by a fire as the priests dug a large hole in the frozen ground. They lined the hole with sacred red earth, then placed cups, pots and food in it for the girl to use in the afterlife.

The priests' chanting grew louder. It was time. The chief priest bent down to hand the girl a strong drink. After a few sips, she slipped into unconsciousness and died. Her body was gently wrapped in thick cloth and laid in the tomb.

When a volcano erupted 500 years later, ash fell on Nevado Ampato, melting the ice. In September 1995, scientists studying the damage found the girl's body. It had been mummified by the freezing cold. Her face had decayed but the rest of her body was still in almost perfect condition. ❖

Mountain rescue
The two men who discovered the girl's body carried it down the mountain as fast as they could so that it would not thaw and decay. It is now stored in a freezer at a university in Peru, where it is studied and preserved.

ITALY

Palermo

SICILY

Palermo
This is the largest city on the Italian island of Sicily.

Picnics
Families often made visits to the cemetery a family outing and would take a picnic lunch!

Sicilian mummies

In the Sicilian city of Palermo, an unusual, centuries-old tradition continued right up until the 1920s.

Deep below a Catholic church was an underground cemetery, called a catacomb. It housed the mummified bodies of 6,000 people! Instead of being horrified, locals would often visit the catacomb. In the cool, dark corridors, a child would be unafraid to raise a creaking coffin lid. Inside could be the body of the child's own great-grandmother!

Many of the mummies lie on benches. Labels tell visitors who they are.

Tourist attraction
Today, the mummies of Sicily attract thousands of visitors from all over the world.

Monk
Palermo's first mummies were the bodies of highly respected monks.

The people went to pay their respects to the mummies, to tell them stories and to ask for their advice. They did not find the mummies upsetting because their families had been visiting the cemetery for more than 300 years. It was simply part of ordinary life. They believed the mummies were a link with loved and respected relatives who had died.

Occasionally the visitors would see a hooded figure moving silently among the coffins.

Again they were unafraid. They knew it was just one of the monks who looked after the catacomb.

These bearded and robed priests lived in a monastery next to the church. Since 1599, they had been mummifying the bodies of respected monks. Other people soon discovered what was happening and began asking for their relatives' bodies to be mummified in return for a donation to the church. They dressed the dead person in his or her best clothes before taking the body to the monastery.

Monks
The monks who look after the catacomb today still wear the brown robes they have worn for hundreds of years.

Clothing
The mummies provide us with information about the styles of clothes people wore in the past.

Father da Gubbio
This monk died in 1599. Every year, the monks give him a gentle dusting with a vacuum cleaner.

The mummification process took over a year to complete – but how it was done was kept secret for hundreds of years!

Some of the mummies are quite gruesome to look at. The mummy of Father Silvestro da Gubbio, the oldest mummy of all, has four laughing skulls displayed around it. When Father da Gubbio died, his body was taken to a special cellar, where it lay over clay pipes for a whole year. This allowed all the body fluids to drain away.

These pipes were used to drain the bodies.

After that, the monks laid the body in the hot Sicilian sun to dry out. Then they washed it in vinegar and, last of all, wrapped it in straw and sweet-smelling herbs. In spite of this, Father da Gubbio's mummy today looks more like a dressed skeleton.

As time went by, the monks improved their embalming process. Their new methods included soaking the body in arsenic or milk of magnesia. This left the skin far softer and gave it a more lifelike colour.

The monks stopped mummifying bodies in 1920, but the mummies are still there. Today the monks take tourists around the catacomb. ❖

Soft skin
The mummies made in the 1800s still have their skin and hair today.

Juan Perón
Perón was the president of Argentina, the richest country in South America. Evita was his second wife.

Buenos Aires
Evita was 15 when she went to live alone in Argentina's capital city.

The mummy mystery

On 28 July, 1952, Dr. Pedro Ara received the phone call he had been waiting for. "Come quickly," said an official-sounding voice, "Evita is dying. President Perón is asking for you."

Thunder crashed and rain poured as Dr. Ara hurried through the streets of Argentina's capital, Buenos Aires. After a year's illness, Evita, the president's beautiful young wife, was dying of cancer.

During her life, Evita had won the hearts of the people. She had set up hospitals and helped the poor. She had also made sure that women in Argentina were allowed to vote.

To stay popular, the president had to make sure the people never forgot his wife. He hired Dr. Ara to preserve her body. The president planned to erect a building and call it the Monument to the People. When it was built, Evita would rest there.

At 8:25 p.m., Evita died.

"This way, please." A tearful nurse led Dr. Ara down the long corridors of the presidential home to the quiet, dimly lit room where Evita lay. Immediately, the expert embalmer began his secret work. This was to be his most important project. Evita must look as if she were sleeping peacefully, but her body must be able to last for hundreds of years.

Slowly and carefully, Dr. Ara replaced Evita's blood with glycerol, a thick liquid that would not decay. Then he placed chemicals in her coffin to kill any insects or bacteria that might attack the body. By dawn the first stage was completed.

Evita was a passionate speaker loved by many Argentinians.

Evita

Evita was born Maria Eva Duarte, the youngest child in a poor family. She later became a popular actress. It was during this time that she met Juan Perón.

Sleeping beauty
People flocked to see Evita's body. Many people dressed in black or wore their best clothes as a sign of respect.

Evita's body was dressed in a white gown and placed in a glass-topped coffin. It was now ready to go on display to the public, who wanted to say farewell.

For 16 days, people lined up along the streets of Buenos Aires. More than 2,000,000 people filed past the coffin, many weeping and bending to kiss the glass lid.

But Dr. Ara began to worry. The glass case was opened twice to wipe away mist on the inside. It was not good for air to get to the body. The doctor knew he must start the next stage of the embalming process.

Evita looked very sick when she died. She weighed only 32 kg (70 pounds). But the embalming process made her look healthy again.

At Dr. Ara's insistence, the coffin was taken to his laboratory. There the body was repeatedly soaked in a bath of chemicals and injected with yet more preservatives. Finally, it was covered in a thin layer of clear plastic.

It took Dr. Ara a year to complete the work, but he was happy. He knew that the body would last forever.

Meanwhile, life in Argentina had become unsettled. President Perón had been overthrown by the army and forced to leave the country.

The new ruler, President Aramburu, did not want anything around that might encourage Perón's supporters. He cancelled the plans for the Monument to the People. He also wanted to get rid of Evita's body, but he was not sure if the body was really hers.

Nation in grief
People had to wait hours to see Evita's body. The huge crowds stretched for 5 kilometres (3 miles).

Floral tribute
Many people brought floral wreaths to lay near Evita's coffin. The day after she died all the flower shops in Buenos Aires were sold out.

President Aramburu
This army general became president of Argentina after Perón fled the country.

The musical
Evita's life is remembered in many books and in musical stage and film productions.

"It looks like a wax model," said an army officer inspecting the mummy. He checked the fingerprints. Then he had her body X-rayed. It was Evita. In fact, Dr. Ara's work was so good that even her internal organs were preserved!

President Aramburu did not want to upset the people by destroying Evita's body. It had to go – but where?

Colonel Koenig, head of Army Intelligence, offered help. Shortly afterwards, in November 1955, the body disappeared.

Many stories began to circulate around Argentina about what had happened to Evita's body. Some said it had been burned, others said it was in her family's graveyard.

Then, in 1970, President Aramburu was murdered. After his death, his lawyer handed over an envelope that solved the mystery.

In September 1971, gravediggers at an Italian cemetery were told to open the tomb of a woman called Maria Maggi de Magistris.

Inside the tomb was a perfectly preserved body. But the body was not Maria Maggi. It was Evita Perón! The body had been secretly buried there 14 years earlier.

In 1974, Evita's body was returned to Argentina. Her long journey ended 24 years after her death when, in 1976, she was laid to rest in her family tomb. The attempt to get rid of her had failed. Today she is more famous than ever – a legend around the world. ❖

Resting place
Evita's body now rests in Recoleta Cemetery in Buenos Aires. It is said to lie in a bombproof compartment.

Together again
In 1974, when Juan Perón died, he was not embalmed. His closed coffin was displayed next to Evita's open one.

Evita's good works have never been forgotten.

Mummy paint
Mummies were once used to make a brown artists' pigment called *Caput Mortuum*, which means "dead head" in Latin.

Mummies today

Today's fascination with mummies began when the French general Napoleon Bonaparte invaded Egypt in 1798. Teams of French scholars began to study the ancient Egyptian civilization.

But much of the evidence had already been destroyed. Thousands of mummies had been burned as fuel, ground up for medicine or simply left to decay.

The first mummies transported to the West were treated little better. Many were "unwrapped" during exhibitions, destroying vital information in the process.

Today most scientists treat the ancient dead respectfully and make the information they find widely available.

Scientists use mummies to find out what diseases people suffered from in the past. They use microscopes to look at skin, bone and other body tissues.

Advances in technology have allowed people to take better care of ancient finds. In 1895, X-rays were discovered. An X-ray picture shows scientists what is inside a mummy case. Mummies no longer need to be unwrapped to be studied.

Aches and pains
This X-ray of an Inca mummy shows that the brain has shrunk to a small round ball at the base of the skull.

A mummy about to enter a CAT scanner

Nowadays, scientists use electronic scanners, called CAT scanners, to produce three-dimensional images of a mummy inside its bandages.

A peep inside
This CAT scan shows the skin on a mummy's face. At another setting, the machine could show the bone below the skin.

Ever present
Before he died in 1832, philosopher Jeremy Bentham arranged for his skeleton to be clothed and his head to be mummified.

While scientists study ancient mummies, funeral directors today are still preserving bodies.

Many people wish to see their dead relatives before the burial. The bodies are embalmed so that they will last a short while. They are not intended to last forever.

Evita Perón's mummy is not the only recent mummy made to last, however. As in ancient Egyptian times, today's mummies are the bodies of rich or famous people.

Thousands of tourists still line up to see the mummy of Vladimir Lenin, the Russian revolutionary leader who died in 1924.

In the USA, people can pay to have their bodies frozen in liquid nitrogen. They do this in the hope that people living in the future will be able to bring them back to life.

This science is called cryogenics. People use freezing temperatures in the same way that ice has preserved many mummies. It is already possible to bring frozen bacteria back to life. However, there is no guarantee that scientists will be able to do the same to people – yet. ❖

Cryogenics
When people choose to be frozen after death, their bodies are preserved in large steel containers.

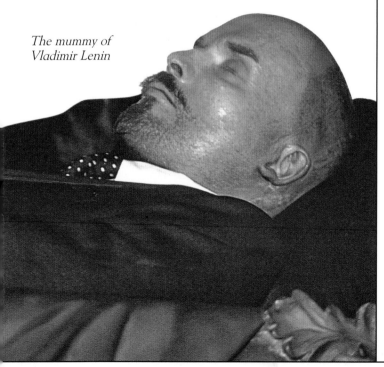

The mummy of Vladimir Lenin

Sci-fi
Science fiction writers and movie-makers capture our imaginations with their ideas about how cryogenics might be used in the future.

Glossary

Afterlife
A life experienced after death. Different cultures have different beliefs about the afterlife.

Altar
A table, rock, or platform used in religious services.

Ancient Egyptians
The people living in Egypt when it was ruled by pharaohs. This was between around 3000 BC and 300 BC.

Artefact
A human-made object found at the sites of ancient homes or graves.

Bacteria
Small, one-celled organisms. Some species cause disease or break down dead matter.

CAT scanner
A computerized scanning machine that produces three-dimensional images of a person's bones and organs.

Catacomb
An underground cemetery.

Cryogenics
The process of storing bodies at very low temperatures so they cannot deacy.

Curse
A wish or spell intended to cause harm to another person.

Embalm
To use chemicals, perfumes or ointments to preserve a body.

Hieroglyph (HIE-row-gliff)
A picture or symbol used to stand for a word or sound in ancient Egyptian writing.

Inca
A South American civilization that flourished from about 1200 to 1532, when it was conquered by the Spaniards.

Litter
A bed, or stretcher, attached to poles. It is used to carry people or mummies.

Llama
A South American animal related to the camel. It is used for meat, wool and transportation.

Monk
A man living and working in a religious community.

Mummify
The process of making a body into a mummy.

Mummy
A body that has been preserved by nature or by people.

Natron
A naturally forming salt used by the ancient Egyptians to absorb fluids.

Pharaoh (FAIR-oh)
The title given to the kings of ancient Egypt who reigned from around 3000 BC to 300 BC.

Sacrifice
To kill a person or animal in a ceremony because of a belief that it will please a god.

Shrine
A cabinet for holding a person's remains; also a place where people honour the memory of a dead person.

Tomb
A grave, monument or small building where a dead body is stored.

Tutankhamun
(Toot-an-KARM-un)
A boy pharaoh who ruled Egypt from about 1336 BC to 1327 BC. He was probably around 16 years old when he died.

Underworld
The ancient Egyptians believed that everyone had to travel through this world beneath the Earth on their journey to the afterlife.

X-rays
Special rays that can pass through only the soft parts of the body. They are used to produce an image of a person's bones and internal organs.